IONA

PAST AND PRESENT

WITH MAPS

RITCHIE

PRINTERS AND PUBLISHERS

GEO. STEWART & CO. LTD., EDINBURGH

1930

PREFACE

WITH the help of our neighbours we have prepared this Map of Iona in order that many of the old Place-names rapidly falling into disuse may be preserved.

We owe much to Mr D. Munro Fraser, Emeritus H.M.C.I.S., for the infinite pains he has taken to make the Map a success, and also for the Appendix containing a translation of the names. He joins us in expressing thanks to Professor W. J. Watson, Edinburgh, for valuable suggestions.

We are grateful to Professor Jehu, Edinburgh, for his fascinating sketch of the Geology of the island. Through the courtesy of the Royal Society of Edinburgh his Map is incorporated in this book.

Mr James Gillespie, L.R.I.B.A. Edinburgh, is thanked for expert assistance in connection with the description of the Ecclesiastical Antiquities.

A. AND E. RITCHIE.

IONA, 1928.

PREFACE TO NEW EDITION

THE welcome already accorded to this book induces us to re-issue it under a title more appropriate to its contents.

ALEC RITCHIE.
EUPHEMIA RITCHIE.

IONA, 1930.

IONA

"Tha Itaca, Cìprus, Ròds
  Ionmhuinn le Clann nam fonn ;
Ach I-Chaluim-Chille, 's i gràdh gach filidh
  Chaidh altrum an Alba nan sonn."
              —SHERIFF NICOLSON.

"Jerusalem, Athens, and Rome
  Are names to the Muses dear,
But sweeter still doth Icolmkill
  Fall on a Scottish ear."

IONA, most musical of sounds, is Alba's Holy of Holies. *I Chaluim-Chille*—as the island is called in the Gaelic tongue—brings us at once into contact with Columba, the originator of its fame. Here the Apostle of the Celts, undeterred by bleak surroundings and savage opponents, raised the first temple to the glory of God. Adamnan, quaintest and best of his early biographers, has in his glowing pages given a wonderful pen-portrait of his great predecessor. He shows a man of deep spirituality, great enthusiasm, and consuming zeal for the souls of men.

Choosing twelve followers, as his Master did before him, Columba in 563 A.D. left his beloved Ireland and set sail in a frail bark (the *Liath Bhalau'h*) over angry western seas, landing at last in a rocky inlet of the Atlantic, named from his hide-covered coracle *Port a' Chu.aich.*

Why should the Saint, who was a born statesman, choose this small island as a centre for his life's labours? Tradition says that Ireland had such a fascination for the missionary that he could not live within sight of its verdant hills,—the longing for his native soil would prove irresistible. Though sentiment had such an influence in his life practical considera-

tions would likely rule his actions.   Islands had attractions for
the founders of the early Celtic Church.   The sea, small though
the vessels of those days were, was the easiest highway.   An
island was by its situation a natural fortress against raiders,
always numerous in a lawless age, and Iona was from its
position a strategic centre for a vigorous evangelical campaign
against surrounding Paganism.   Dalriada, in Argyllshire, was
already in possession of Irish emigrants, who, in the previous
century had seized this territory nearest to their own kingdom.
An early writer states that the island was a gift to Columba
from King Conall in 565.   How much Columba's labours
were blest is well known to all students of history.   His royal
descent gave him authority before which kings bowed their
heads, and even Brude, King of the Picts, an obstinate
monarch living near Inverness, is said to have accepted the
faith of Jesus Christ.   Aidan, Conall's successor, we know was
admitted to the Dalriadic throne with Christian rites by the
hand of Columba.   The Coronation stone then used (the
"Liath Fail" or stone of destiny) is said to be the one that
was stolen from Scone and that is now in Westminster Abbey,
—the sacred seat on which British monarchs are crowned.

But Iona became not merely "the luminary of the Caledonian
regions," its candle dispersed the darkness of heathendom from
the rude Northumbrians.   Missionaries from its shores made
the plains of Italy, the mountains of Switzerland, and the
table lands of France seminaries of religious activity, where
culture was prized and science not neglected.   No name is
more loved, no character more reverenced than that of the
Royal Saint who brought the Evangel to our Western Land
and kindled therein a torch that has never been put out.

St Columba was called to rest on the 9th day of June 597
after transcribing with feeble hand the thirty-fourth Psalm
at the verse : "they that seek the Lord shall not want any good
thing."   Historians note that the same year saw the landing
of St Augustine in Kent.   About 165 years before, St Ninian,
the Apostle of the Southern Picts, had died at Whithorn.
St Kentigern, the Apostle of Strath-Clyde, was a contemporary
of Columba, and met him towards the close of his life..

So eager was King Oswald of Northumbria to benefit by associating with the Sacred Family or "Muinntir" of Iona that he became a student of theology in the island. When he resumed the sceptre he invited Aidan, a zealous missionary, to visit his palace. The eloquence of this messenger was so persuasive that the monastery of Lindisfarne, "the Iona of the East," became a centre of Christian influence over all the Northern counties of England.

Among the early scholars of St Columba's time and later there must have been craftsmen of rare ability, judging from the specimens of their handicraft in our museums. They excelled in metal work and in enamelling. They were masters in the art of illumination. The Book of Kells, now in Trinity College, Dublin, and the Lindisfarne Gospels in the British Museum are among the finest examples of their illuminated work. The designs, the colours and the lettering are marvellous. It is inconceivable how the human eye could see and the pen execute the minute and intricate patterns with which these MSS. are decorated.

A legend of peculiar beauty, associated with St Brendan, tells of the wanderings of those early monks who went in search of that far away "Tir nan og," a land beyond the Hebridean seas, an isle from which old age was banished and where the dwellers enjoyed eternal youth.

With the exception of the *Vallum* situated to the north-west of the Cathedral and which may be pre-Christian, and that other landmark *Carn-Cul-ri-Eirinn*, there are no visible remains associated with St Columba.

From Adamnan we gather that the dwellings of the monks were of the daub and wattle type. Probably these lay to the north of the present Abbey, near where the big boulder (*a'Chlach mhor*) lies.

On landing at St Ronan's Bay (adjoining the present pier) the visitor will observe a sandy beach at a short distance to the south. This is the far famed *Martyrs' Bay*; and as late as the days of Pennant (1771), "a broad paved road called *Sraid nam marbh* (Street of the Dead) led hence round the back of the Nunnery to the burial ground." In this bay the "illustrious" dead were landed, and one can still see the little mound (the *Ealadh*) where the bier was placed, ere it was borne to the *Reilig Odhrain*.

THE NUNNERY.

The ruins of the Nunnery are situated about a quarter of a mile south of the Abbey. The community, which was originally of the Benedictine Order, was founded in 1203 by Reginald Macdonald, Lord of the Isles. The Deed of Confirmation still exists at the Vatican. The effigy of Anna, the last Prioress, with an inscription bearing the date 1543, is preserved in St Ronan's Chapel which adjoins the Nunnery. The ruins are grouped round a quadrangle which formed the Cloister Garth, with the Convent Church in the usual position on the north side; the Chapter House and other apartments on the east side; and the Refectory on the south. Of the buildings forming the western side, only a portion of one wall now remains. The architectural features are early thirteenth century in character, and this interesting group is a good example of the Transition style.

In 1923 the buildings were repaired and the garden in the Cloister Garth was planted by her family in memory of Mrs R. J. Spencer. When the workmen were relaying the floor of the Church, three silver gilt spoons and a gold fillet were discovered wrapt up in what appeared to have been a fragment of cotton cloth. With the exception of the one used at the Coronation, these spoons are supposed to be the oldest of their kind in Britain, dating from the twelfth or thirteenth century. They are beautifully proportioned. One of them is in perfect preservation, and a copy of it can be seen in St Ronan's Chapel. The gold fillet is decorated with a foliaceous pattern. These "finds" are now in the Antiquarian Museum in Edinburgh. St Ronan's Chapel, which probably dates from the fourteenth century, has been roofed over and converted into a museum for housing the carved stones, etc. Another fillet and ring were found when the floor of this building was being relaid. It is believed that St Ronan's was used as the church of the island up to the time of the Reformation.

On the present road to the burial ground stands Maclean's Cross, an example of the fifteenth century solid-headed type peculiar to the West Coast. The shaft of schist is carved on both sides with delicate tracery. Looking at this cross one marvels how it has withstood the exposure of centuries.

The *Reilig Odhrain*, aptly called the Westminster Abbey of Scotland, is claimed by some writers to have been used as a royal burying ground, even before the advent of St Columba! One fact is certain, that for many centuries King and Chief, Noble and Commoner have been buried in this churchyard.

From the pen of Dean Munro who visited Iona in 1549, we get the following graphic account of the Reilig Odhrain :—

"Within the ile of Colmkill, there is ane sanctuary also, or kirkzaird, callit in Erische Religoran quhilk is a very fair Kirkzaird, and weill biggit about with staine and lyme. Into this sanctuary there is three tombes of staine formit like little chapels, with ane braid gray marble or quhin staine in the gavill of ilk ane of the tombes. In the staine of the ane tombe there is written in Latin letters, *Tumulus Regum Scotiae*, that is the tombe ore grave of the Scotts Kinges : within this tombe according to our Scotts and Erische cronikels ther layes fortey-eight crouned Scotts Kinges. The tombe on the South side forsaid hes this inscription, *Tumulus Regum Hyberniae*, that is the tombe of the Irland Kinges—ther wes foure Irland Kinges eirdit in the said tombe. Upon the north syde of ane Scotts tombe, the inscriptione beares *Tumulus Regum Norwegiae*, that is the tombe of the Kings of Norroway—ther layes eight Kings of Norroway . . . becaus it was the maist honorable and ancient place that was in Scotland in thair dayes."

Two historical events stand out in connection with the Reilig Odhrain. Shakespeare refers to it in the play of "Macbeth," when Rosse asks MacDuff where Duncan's body is, and MacDuff makes reply, "carried to Colme-Kill, the sacred store-house of his predecessors, and guardian of their bones." The other reference occurs in the Lord of the Isles, where it is related that Scott's hero, who assisted the Bruce at the battle of

Bannockburn, is buried in the chapel of the enclosure. The Ridge of the Kings and that of the Chiefs exist only since 1868, when the Iona Club collected the monuments and placed them within the present railings for protection. The late James Drummond, R.S.A., in his book entitled "Sculptured Monuments in Iona and the West Highlands," gives beautiful and accurate drawings of the carved slabs and crosses to be found here. If the chapel within the Reilig Odhrain be the one restored by Queen Margaret, then, undoubtedly, it is one of the oldest historical ruins in Scotland. Margaret and Malcolm Canmore visited Iona in 1072 (circa), and it is stated that "the Queen restored the smaller church of Columcille." The doorway of the Chapel is worthy of note. The jambs and capitals are Irish-Romanesque in character, and are similar to many Irish examples dating from the eighth to the eleventh century. The arch is more Norman in style and appears to be later than the jambs. In the interior, a late mediæval tomb has been inserted in the South wall. The canopy of the tomb is surmounted by an ogee arch, with a *Crucifixion* carved at the apex. The recumbent figure is missing but was complete when Pennant visited Iona, and is described by him. Recently the chapel was repaired by Mr George Service and the carved monuments which rested on the floor are now placed temporarily in the South Aisle of the Abbey.

Entering the Cathedral grounds, there is on the left an eminence called "The Abbot's mound" or *Torr Abb*, otherwise called *Dun nam Manach*, supposed by some to be the hill mentioned by Adamnan which St Columba ascended the day before his death. Those who take the view that the original monastery was much further north think this hill was *Cnoc Daraich*, to the west of the Duchess's Cross. Here he blessed Iona and prophesied that in years to come the Island would attract pilgrims from all parts of the world. During the centuries that have passed since his death, this prophecy has been amply fulfilled.

St Martin's Cross, the finest expression of the religious sentiment of that period, embodies in form and in harmony of design a noble conception of the beautiful. The shaft of the

Cross, which is of whinstone, rests on a pedestal of granite. Spirals formed of intertwined vipers and ornamented bosses decorate the front, while Scriptural scenes are depicted on the obverse side, the Virgin and Child with surrounding angels forming the central Panel. One cannot fix accurately the date of this Cross, but in all probability it belongs to the ninth or tenth century.

In the summer of 1927, Professor R. A. S. Macalister had the bottom panel on the obverse side freed from lichen, and discovered a faint inscription in Irish letters which, when translated, reads : " A prayer for Gilla Crist who made this cross."

The broken shaft of St Matthew's Cross faces the Nave door. The *Temptation* can still be distinguished on the front, but in general the decorations are much defaced. St John's Cross stands in front of what is called St Columba's tomb, and since its restoration, by Professor Macalister, one can now see the cross as it was originally and marvel at its unique and superb form and the varied and minute patterns that cover the entire surface. Dr Joseph Anderson in his " Scotland in Early Christian Times " says :—" The Cross Shaft is decorated in the purest style of Celtic art with such inimitable beauty, and intricacy and harmony of design that I am safe in saying of it that no finer specimen of art workmanship exists in Scotland." There is no authority for the statement (unfortunately repeated in one guide book after another) that " at one time there were 360 standing crosses in Iona, many of them having been broken and thrown into the Sound."

The stone from which the Iona slabs and crosses have been hewn is not found in the island ; but was probably brought from the south end of Mull. At a place called *Port an t-Slaoicein*, there are indications of an extensive quarry having been worked there in past times ; anyway the stone is of the same kind, and there is no other locality in the neighbourhood whence blocks similar to the crosses and slabs could have been obtained. A visit to this port is very interesting on account of the peculiar lamination of the strata.

Facing St John's Cross is an ancient burial ground with old Celtic slabs and inscriptions. The little oratory at the end contains two stone cists. Tradition has it that one of these contained the body of St Columba.

THE ABBEY OR CATHEDRAL.

In the long interval that intervened between the simple settlement of Saint Columba and the building of the present Abbey, many erections, first of wood and then of stone, were more than once destroyed by the pagan Norsemen and many of the monks were slain. The present Abbey stands on the site of the one built by Reginald Macdonald in 1203. In 1507, John, Bishop of the Isles, joined Iona to his See and the Abbey Church then became the Cathedral of the Diocese until the Reformation.

The Church, which was dedicated to St Mary, is cruciform in plan, consisting of a Choir with South Aisle, North and South Transepts with a Tower above the Crossing, and the Nave. The Sacristy is on the north side of the Choir. The Cloister which lies to the north of the Nave has the Chapter House and Dormitories on the east side, and the Refectory on the north.

The Abbey or Cathedral shows signs of many alterations, but as the style of the masonry is much the same throughout, it is not easy to distinguish the points of junction of the work of the various periods. With, however, some small exceptions, e.g., the east wall of the North Transept which is late Norman, the building is almost entirely late fifteenth and early sixteenth century work. The greater part of the Nave is quite modern, having been rebuilt or reconstructed in 1905.

The north wall of the Choir shows indications of a Crypt, in which case the Choir floor would then be at a much higher level than at present. Over the west jamb of the Sacristy door, which is a later insertion, there is a column supporting two pointed arches, and it is probable that these arches opened into a Chapel. On the south wall of the Choir the remains of a Piscina and Sedilia can be seen. These are beautifully decorated, but unfortunately the ornament is now much decayed. The monumental slab on the floor of the Choir at one time contained a *Brass* and is the only one of the kind in the west of Scotland : it is ascribed to a Macleod. The little heart-shaped stone with an incised Celtic cross secured within a metal cage is called St Columba's Pillow.

On the east side of the North Transept there are two small chapels and in the niche between them, there was at one time a statue. Above these chapels in the thickness of the wall there is a passage which probably led from the dormitories to the chapel above the Sacristy.

In the Choir there is a well preserved recumbent effigy dated 1500, of Abbot Mackinnon, and the cross dedicated to this Abbot and his father is in the North Transept. The date on the cross is 1489, showing that it was wrought before the death of the Abbot. Only part of the shaft remains and this is decorated with foliaceous spirals springing from the tail of a dragon. The carvings on the capitals of the Abbey pillars are quaint and varied. The craftsmen have introduced a realism into their mystic conceptions of Bible truths, with the result that the subjects are a distinctive feature of the Abbey, and well worth an exclusive study. On the abacus of the south-east capital at the Tower Crossing there was found an inscription in Lombardic letters,—" Donaldus O'Brolchan Fecit Hoc Opus."

Some years ago the foundations of an early South Aisle were discovered outside the southern entrance door of the Abbey, showing fine mouldings of the Transition period.

Recently, H.M. Office of Works partially restored (from fragments found lying about) two of the Cloister arches, and these give an idea how beautiful they must have been when complete. To the north of the retaining wall of the Abbey enclosure are the ruins of what once was the Bishop's House, and on the south can be seen the ruins of St Mary's Chapel.

About 200 yards west of *Port an Diseirt* is the foundation of an early church. A trilothan adjoins it ; the top stone of which was removed many years ago. In this same field

there is the granite boulder previously mentioned, a relic of
the Ice Age and called St Columba's Table.

Here it should be mentioned that all the ecclesiastical buildings in Iona were gifted in 1899 to Trustees for the Church
of Scotland by George, eighth Duke of Argyll. His Grace's
monument and that of the Dowager Duchess are in the South
Transept of the Abbey.

Leaving the precincts of the Cathedral and proceeding
north you cross the Mill stream used in post-Columban days
in connection with the grinding of the corn. To the left of
the road is the *Vallum* (with Fosse), still well defined, which,
as already stated, probably goes back to prehistoric times.
A little to the west of the Vallum is the *Lochan Mor*. The
ground it covered was drained about a century ago. The
causeway running at right angles may have acted as a boundary
to retain the water and as a pathway across the marsh. About
a quarter of a mile to the west of the Lochan Mor is the
site of the *Cobhain Cuildich* (Hermit's Cell), now reduced to a
circle of stones.

Dun I is the highest hill on the Island (332 feet). The
cairn on the top was erected in 1897 to commemorate the
1300th anniversary of St Columba's death. To the north east
is the "Well of Age," still associated with certain harmless
ceremonies. The view from the top of this hill on a clear
day can hardly be surpassed. To the west stretches the un-
bounded Atlantic. Sweeping in a circle to the north west are
seen Barra Head, Tiree, Coll, Rum, Eigg, and the Coolins,
and the higher mountains on the mainland, Mull with its
towering Ben More and winding sea lochs. Turning to the
south we see Jura with its three Paps, Colonsay and Islay. An
inner circle to the north embraces the Treshnish group, the
"far-famed Staffa" among them, and many other islands. At
one time, a number of the islands included in the Treshnish
group (such as Lunga) were inhabited, but now, they are only
the home of the sea bird and the wandering seal. These
islands have an individual beauty and character, and a visit
to one or all of them on a fine summer's day is an experience
never to be forgotten.

From the top of Dun I one can see the size and character
of Iona. Roughly speaking the island is 3½ miles long by
1½ miles broad. Cultivated slopes stretch along the eastern
side and through the centre of the island. Rugged knolls and
moorland extend north and south in striking contrast to the
arable land, which shows up like a chequer board of varied
green.

Stretching almost from the foot of Dun I are the famous
White Sands, composed chiefly of the shells of small land
snails. They lie, dazzling the gaze, in gentle undulations, and,
as the sea runs in, the lower reaches become pellucid mysteries
of green, changing to deep purple where the beds of tangle
sway with the tide.

Bishop Knox in 1609 summoned the West Highland Chiefs
to meet him at Iona, on the *Iomair nan Achd*, and there, if not
on the sacred "Black stones of Hy," they subscribed to the
Nine Statutes of Iona, drawn up for the better government
of the Hebrides. Tradition, however, says there was only *one*
stone, which was destroyed early in the 18th Century by a
fanatic who believed that it bewitched the people.

When Sir Walter Scott visited Iona in 1811, "he counted
forty cottages in front of the Nunnery." Within the last thirty
years the thatched cottage has practically disappeared and
has been replaced for the most part by substantial houses of
two storeys.

Apart from its ecclesiastical and historical interest, the
island has a great natural charm for the lover of the wilder
aspects of nature. *Port a' Churaich* lies at the extreme south
where St Columba landed. There is a slightly raised mound
at the head of the bay where his coracle is said to have been
buried. The mound is about 60 feet long. On the old beach,
to the right of Port a' Churaich, there are a number of rather
curious piles of stone, varying in size : what their object, or
what meaning, if any, was attached to them, no one can tell!

The news of the Battle of Waterloo was first heard in
these regions by the inhabitants of a small hamlet that clustered
on the slope above Port a' Churaich. One can still make out
the site of this settlement.

Going westward we come to *Port Laraichean*, the "Bay of the Sites." A more or less artificial rampart protects the bay from observation, and the remains of circular dwellings are still to be traced on the flat plateau immediately above the bay. In the opinion of the archæologist these sites may be pre-Christian.

On the highest ridge of this part of the Island is Carn Cul ri Eirinn, the most touching link with St Columba, who on landing, climbed the hill, and finding he could no longer see his beloved country had the cairn erected. ˙

The coast line of the southern part is varied by fine bold headlands and rocks massed together in fantastic form, great deep fissures, where the waves rush in, making weird sounds that startle the explorer. These again give place to bays of exquisite beauty, where many coloured pebbles present a mosaic of inimitable colour. Against the cliff, on the south west side of the Machair, the Spouting Cave at half-tide sends up a volume of spray, which often takes strange shapes as it drifts over the headland.

A very beautiful green knoll on the left hand side of the road just before entering the Machair is called the *Sithean Mor* (the big fairy-hill). Here, the Chronicle says, St Columba communed with the angels. Hence it often goes by the name of *Cnoc nan Aingeal*, the Hill of the Angels. Many years ago there was a circle of stones on the top of the "Shian": no trace of them now remains.

We cannot leave the west without drawing attention to the two magnificent headlands *Eilean Didil* and *Corr-Eilean* that face the Atlantic,—grim bulwarks defying the storms, and sheltering between them two beautiful bays *Pollarain* and *Port Bàn*.

Iona is an ideal centre for short excursions, and the choice is almost bewildering. On a fine day the magic of sea and land call irresistibly, and perhaps those strange and almost exotic group of Islands, the Treshnish Isles, rouse most the curiosity and the longing of the explorer. Among them are the Cairnburg Islands (*Mor* and *Beag*) with their astonishing ramparts still showing the remains of extensive fortifications.

Seeing them one can believe in the old Gaelic saying,—" Co traing ri dorsair an Cairnburg," " As busy as a Cairnburg sentinel or doorkeeper."

In the vicinity are those havens of seal and bird life—Lunga and the Dutchman's Cap, and lastly far famed Staffa. Nearer home are Erraid, Eilean Chalman, Soa and others, all interesting in their way. Among those islets one gets very close to undisturbed nature, and a vision of these Hebridean gems, shimmering under an unclouded sky, will often come back with a refreshing vividness, when the toilers return to the drab realities of the city.

A. and E. R.

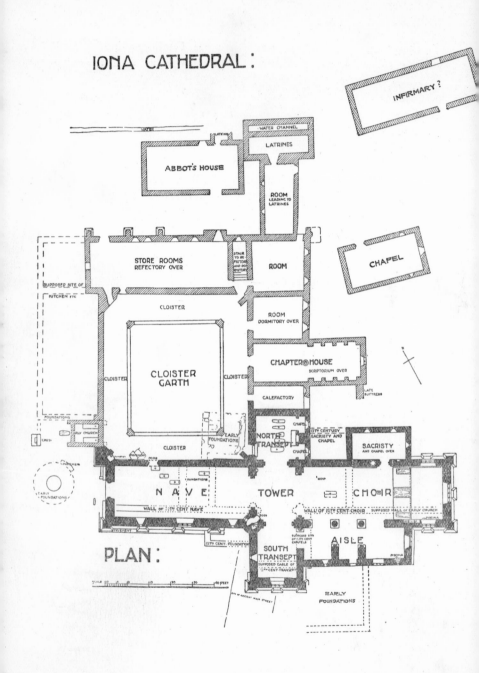

IONA CATHEDRAL:

INFIRMARY?

WATER CHANNEL
LATRINES

ABBOT'S HOUSE

ROOM
LEADING TO
LATRINES

STORE ROOMS
REFECTORY OVER

STAIR
TO BE
REFECTORY
AND DORMITORY

ROOM

CHAPEL

SUPPOSED SITE OF
KITCHEN ETC

CLOISTER

ROOM
DORMITORY OVER

CLOISTER
GARTH

CLOISTER

CHAPTER HOUSE
SCRIPTORIUM OVER

CLOISTER

LATE
BUTTRESS

CALEFACTORY

FOUNDATIONS

EARLY CHURCH

EARLY
FOUNDATIONS

CHAPEL

NORTH
TRANSEPT

13TH CENTURY
SACRISTY AND
CHAPEL

SACRISTY
AND CHAPEL OVER

CLOISTER

CHAPEL

EARLY
FOUNDATIONS

FOUNDATIONS

N A V E

TOWER

C H O I R

WALL OF 13TH CENT NAVE

WALL OF 13TH CENT CHOIR

SUPPOSED WALL OF EARLY CHURCH

PISCINA

13TH CENT FOUNDATIONS

SOUTH
TRANSEPT

SUPPOSED SITE
OF 13TH CENT
CHAPELS

A I S L E

PISCINA

PLAN:

SUPPOSED GABLE OF
13TH CENT TRANSEPT

EARLY
FOUNDATIONS

SCALE 0 10 20 30 40 FEET

SITE OF ANCIENT MAIN STREET

CATHEDRAL   IONA   St ORAN'S CHAPEL

St MARTIN'S CROSS

St JOHN'S CROSS

McLean's Cross—15th Century

Mackinnon's Cross, Iona 1489

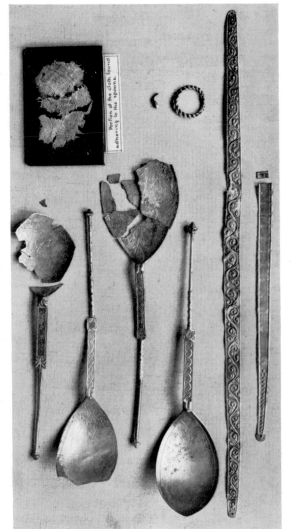

Portion of the cloth found adhering to the spoons.

SILVER GILT SPOONS, FIBULAS AND RING (GOLD) FOUND IN NUNNERY

IONA

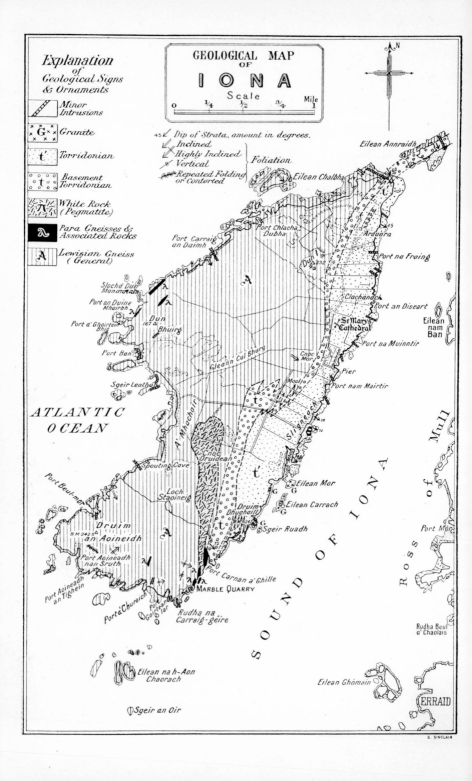

GEOLOGICAL MAP
OF
IONA
Scale
0   ¼   ½   ¾   1   Mile

Explanation
of
Geological Signs
& *Ornaments*

Minor Intrusions
×G× Granite
t' Torridonian
Basement Torridonian
White Rock (Pegmatite)
λ Para Gneisses & Associated Rocks
Λ Lewisian Gneiss (General)

45 Dip of Strata, amount in degrees.
Inclined
Highly Inclined
Vertical   } Foliation
Repeated Folding or Contorted

N

ATLANTIC
OCEAN

Eilean Annraidh
Eilean Chalbha
Port Chlacha Dubha
Port Carraig an Daimh
Arduara
Port na Fraing
Slochd Dun Mananain
Port an Duine Mharbh
Clachanach
Port an Diseart
Port a'Ghoirtein Bhig
Dun 167△ Bhuirg
St Mary's Cathedral
Eilean nam Ban
Port Ban
Gleann Cùl Bhuirg
Cnoc Mòr
Port na Muinntir
Sgeir Leathan
Pier
Maol
Port nam Mairtir
A'Mhachair
Slignéach
Spouting Cave
Cnoc Druidean
Loch Staoineig
Eilean Mòr
Eilean Carrach
Druim Dhughaill
Druim an Aoineadh
λ
Sgeir Ruadh
Port Aoineadh nan Sruth
t'
Port Carnan a'Ghille
MARBLE QUARRY
Port Aoineadh an Tighein
Port a'Churaich
Port Goirtean Iar
Rudha na Carraig-géire
Eilean na h-Aon Chaorach
Eilean Ghòmain
Sgeir an Oir
ERRAID

SOUND OF IONA
Ross of Mull
Port Mòr
Rudha Beul a' Chaolais

G. SINCLAIR

A SKETCH OF THE GEOLOGY OF IONA

By PROFESSOR T. J. JEHU

To the historian Iona is celebrated for its ecclesiastical remains, and venerated as the centre of St Columba's activities in Scotland.

To the geologist the island makes its appeal on account of the great antiquity of the rocks of which it is made up. For the most part these belong to the oldest geological formations of which we have any record. They form a part of what have been termed the "foundation stones" of Scotland, and indeed of the whole of Britain. The time of their formation carries us back to the pre-Cambrian era which antedates sediments in which fossils are found. At this early stage in the history of the earth's crust, it may safely be said that any life forms that may have existed were so primitive that they could leave no definite trace on the sands of time. The whole story of the evolution of life as recorded in the rocks of the earth's crust belongs to the long eras which followed the formation of nearly all the rocks of Iona.

The western and greater part of Iona is composed of rocks belonging to the Archæan or Lewisian Complex of Gneisses. These are overlain on the eastern margin by altered sediments of Torridonian age. Both belong to pre-Cambrian times. Apart from these, the only other formations represented to a very small extent are (1) minor igneous intrusions related to the Ross of Mull granite, referable to the Lower Old Red Sandstone period of igneous activity, (2) igneous dykes belonging to the Tertiary period of igneous activity which is responsible for the great lava fields of Mull, (3) glacial erratics carried chiefly from the Ross of Mull during the Great

Ice Age, and (4) raised-beach deposits of Late-Glacial and Post-Glacial age. Areas of blown sand at the north end of the island and on the western side, especially on the plain of the Machair, together with recent beach deposits, belong to modern times.

Rocks of the Archæan Complex occupy about three-quarters of the island and extend under the sea to the Isle of Soa. The greater part of them are altered igneous rocks now in the form of gneisses. The banding of these gneisses, though somewhat irregular, follows on the whole the direction of the main trend of the island with dips to the south of east. This conforms with the general strike and dip of the succeeding Torridonian sediments along the eastern side of the island. Amongst the gneisses a granitic type is on the whole predominant. This is grey or pink in colour with bands of varying thickness of light-coloured quartz and felspar alternating with thinner and darker bands chiefly of hornblende. Occasionally darker gneisses or schists occur, sometimes fine-grained, forming hornblende schists, at other times coarser in texture yielding hornblende crystals an inch or more in length. At places the old gneisses show a considerable development of epidote of a greenish or yellowish colour occurring irregularly or as films and again sometimes as bands up to a thickness of between 1 and 2 feet.

Here and there amongst the gneisses (orthogneisses) which represent altered igneous rocks examples of highly altered sediments (paragneisses) are found. On the north-western coast opposite Sloc Dun Mhanannain, bands of marble are seen associated with graphite-bearing rocks and garnet-biotite-granulites. The graphite is associated at one locality with abundant pyrites and the presence of the latter is sometimes indicated by marked rusty weathering. Further inland, about 300 yards N.N.E. of the summit of Dun Bhuirg, there is a band of beautiful marble locally known as the "Silver Stone." It is pinkish grey in colour, mottled green by serpentine, and rich in silvery flakes of talc. Some garnet-biotite-granulites near the extreme south-western part of the island, to the east and west of Druim an Aoinidh, may also possibly represent altered sediments. A small band of white tremolite marble occurs just west of Maol close to the junction of the gneisses with the Torridonian conglomerate. Another band of marble occurs a little way inland from Port a'Churaich.

The best known area showing the presence of these ancient Archæan sediments is at the Marble Quarry on the south coast. Here, in association with the marble, a series of very fine-grained greenish rocks occur which are in part at any rate of sedimentary origin. The Iona marble is a serpentinous marble of peculiar beauty, the white calcareous portions being streaked and mottled by yellowish green serpentine. The marble outcrops in a nearly vertical band about 20 feet thick at its seaward termination. It cannot be followed far inland.

These sediments, though they form but a minor proportion of the Lewisian Complex, are of intense interest to geologists as being the oldest representatives of that class of rocks found in Britain. The graphite which some of them contain has probably been formed from carbonaceous material entombed in the original sediments, and this material possibly indicates the presence of some form of early plant life. The marbles or altered limestones, though they contain no trace of fossils, may possibly, but not necessarily, indicate some early forms of calcareous plants or animals.

The latest members of the Archæan Complex are veins or bands of pegmatite (usually comparatively unaltered) of varying width which often cut across the banding of the gneisses. The veins are usually pink in colour and rather coarse in texture and consist chiefly of quartz and felspar. They represent igneous intrusions into the gneisses, formed in pre-Torridonian times. One of these later pegmatites is seen to cut the Iona Marble at the quarry. An unusual and peculiar type of these pegmatites deserves mention as it forms a special feature in the topography of the island. It is known as the "White Rock" and can be traced from the Marble Quarry inland for over a mile. At its northern end it swells out and stands higher than the rocks on either side overlooking the Machair in the form of old sea cliffs belonging to the epoch at which some of the ancient raised beaches were formed.

The nature of this rock has been somewhat of a puzzle
to geologists. It consists for the most part of felspar, the
individual crystals of which are very shattered, and it probably
represents a huge pegmatite vein. Since its formation it has
suffered much from earth movements and has undergone
silicification accompanied by the formation of epidote. Its
base round the northern extremity and on either side is marked
by the presence of greenish mashed rocks.

The Lewisian or Archæan Rocks were foliated and rendered
gneissic in pre-Torridonian times as proved by the occurrence
of boulders and pebbles of the gneisses in the basement Torridonian beds.

A vast interval of time is represented by the unconformable
junction between the Lewisian and the overlying Torridonian
rocks. During this interval the Archæan rocks of the west
of Scotland, now exposed along the western seaboard of
Sutherland and Ross, in Rona, in the northern part of Raasay,
in Coll, Tiree, Iona, and the whole of the Outer Hebrides,
formed a land surface, which was probably part of a continent
extending across the northern Atlantic. This land was carved
into hills and valleys, and on this uneven surface the succeeding
Torridonian sediments were laid down. In Sutherland and
Ross the Torridonian beds consist to a large extent of red sand-
stones, typical of a continental area and of desert conditions.
In Iona argillaceous or clayey beds are more prominent and
all the Torridonian is more altered or metamorphosed by
subsequent movements and by the intrusion of the Ross of
Mull granite at a later period. These Torridonian beds form
a belt on the eastern side stretching from the islet of Eilean
Annraidh, of which they constitute the greater part, south-
westwards to the southern margin, east of Port Carnan a'Ghille.
They can be arranged in two main divisions—

    (2) Upper or Flaggy Group—consisting of rapid alterna-
        tions of sandy and shaly material sometimes in the
        form of imperfect slates and flagstones.

    (1) Lower or Basement Group—Breccias, conglomerates,
        arkoses, and grits, with argillaceous bands especially
        in the upper part.

The conglomerate at the base is largely made up of fragments derived from the underlying Archæan rocks. At the north-east end of the island a remarkably coarse breccia with boulders as large as one's head is seen to repose on the Archæan rocks. Highly inclined flagstones dipping towards the Sound run along the east coast and are well seen at the landing stage. A few pegmatite veins of later age than those previously mentioned are seen traversing the Torridonian beds.

The Archæan and Torridonian rocks of Iona have suffered from intense movements which took place most probably in post-Cambrian times and which resulted in the well known thrust planes of Sutherland and Ross. It has been suggested that the great Moine Thrust of the North-west Highlands runs along the line of the Sound of Iona, separating the Torridonian of that island from the Moine gneiss found in Mull to the east of the Ross granite. This is by no means proved, but if it be the case, the thrust plane must have been formed prior to the intrusion of that granite.

The next event in the history of the area as recorded in the rocks is the intrusion of the Ross of Mull granite. This granite was formed by an igneous magma cooling at great depths below the surface during Lower Old Red Sandstone times, and is of about the same age as the well known granites of Ben Nevis, Etive, and the Southern Uplands. It is now exposed at the surface owing to the wearing away during the course of subsequent ages of the rocks under which it was buried. The period to which it belongs was one of great igneous activity in Scotland and the lavas which were then poured out at the surface are now well represented in the Lorne district, in the Sidlaws and Ochils, in the Pentland Hills, and in the Cheviots. Every visitor to Iona is struck by the colour contrast of pink and grey presented by the rocks of the two shores,—the pink granite of the Ross on the one hand and the grey flagstones of the Torridonian on the other. The granite itself must underlie parts of the Sound, for it appears above the waters close to the coastline of Iona in skerries that are partly hidden under seaweed. The skerries are known as Eilean Mor, Eilean Carrach, and Sgeir Ruadh.

Genetically connected with the granite of the Ross of Mull
are a number of minor igneous intrusions of varying character
which here and there penetrate the older rocks of Iona. The
most conspicuous of these is a brick red felsitic sheet cutting
the old rocks to the north-west of the Machair and south-east
of Dun Bhuirg.

The huge mass of the Ross of Mull granite intervenes
between the Torridonian rocks of Iona and the Moine schists
of western Mull which are also of pre-Cambrian age. The
heat and pressure due to the intrusion has affected the rocks
on either side, hardening them and producing new contact
minerals of various kinds, especially black mica.

A lapse of time, which on a conservative estimate amounts
to many millions of years, intervenes between the Ross of Mull
intrusion and the age of any other later rocks found in Iona.
This interval embraces the Carboniferous period and the closing
period of the Palæozoic, together with the whole of the Mesozoic
Era (of which, however, there are representative beds in Mull
underlying the basaltic lava flows).

During early Tertiary times what is now the west of
Scotland was the site of volcanic phenomena on a stupendous
scale. The lavas ejected at this time are well seen in the
terraced cliffs of Mull, and indeed form the greater part of
that island, associated with various types of igneous intrusions.
Remnants of the lava flows are well exposed in Staffa and
the Treshnish Isles. The very name of Staffa—Island of
Staves (Norse)—is derived from the two tiers of columns
belonging to a basalt lava which have made the island famous.
Red volcanic ash emerges from beneath the western margin
of the lava. The age of these volcanic flows was determined
in 1851 by the wonderful Leaf Beds, discovered by the Duke
of Argyll, formed in a pool during an interval between two flows
and now exposed on the cliffs at Ardtun beyond Bunessan.
Another interesting relic of this age is the upright tree discovered
long ago by Macculloch, embedded in the lava in a coastal cliff
of the Gribun peninsula. The only evidences of this great
volcanic period still remaining in Iona are the igneous dykes
of basalt seen cutting all the older rocks at various localities

in the island. These usually run in a north-west direction and represent cracks in the earth's crust infilled from below by the uprise of lava. They are frequently exposed along the coastline. A good example is seen on the foreshore just north of Port a'Mhuilinn, north-east of the Cathedral ; another may be noted on the shore just north of the Argyll Hotel ; and still another on the west side of Traigh Mhor. Further examples may be noted along the south and west coasts.

Subsequent to the events just mentioned but prior to the Glacial Period the region must have undergone subsidence as evinced by the hundred-foot raised beach of Mull and the neighbouring islets. The Dutchman's Cap owes its characteristic form to the marine erosion that took place when the land stood about 100 feet lower than it does at present. " The brim of the Cap marks the level reached by the waves at that time and the crown is the island that then stood above the sea." At that time a considerable part of what is now Iona must have been submerged and the sea extended right across the middle of the present island. No clear traces in the way of deposits formed at the time of this submergence are now left. A re-emergence of the land was followed by the oncoming of cold climatic conditions culminating in the Great Ice Age. No boulder clay has been observed in the island, but some rubbly glacial drift mantles the surface at places, as for instance on the sloping ground between Dun I and the Cathedral. The rocky hummocks which doubtless owe their form to the erosion of glaciers are now so weathered that ice markings have been obliterated. But clear evidence of the over-riding of the island by an ice-sheet streaming from the south-east is afforded by boulders of the red Ross of Mull granite which occur in great profusion all over the island. Many of these have been used as building materials and for the construction of stone dykes. A mass weighing many tons lies high up on the north-western side of Dun I ; and many huge boulders are seen near the eastern shore, such as that lying just north of Port na Fraing. During Late Glacial times a submergence took place again resulting in a considerable reduction of the area of the island. Beaches belonging to this epoch are well developed on the east side of Iona, and again on the west side, indicating that Iona must have been nearly constricted at the middle into two isles for a time. Embayments of the 50-foot beach with well-marked old sea cliffs can be seen on the inner side of the plain of the Machair, one of these passing into the steep, narrow, strath-like depression of Gleann Cul Bhuirg, north of An Teampull. Another ancient sea cliff is well seen off the east coast running north from Traigh nan Siolag.

These oscillations of level continued into Post-Glacial times as shown by remnants of a 25-foot raised beach at various places. At Clachanach the inner angle of this beach lies at present about 20 feet above the sea, and south of the United Free Church, and again north of Dun Bhuirg, similar levels can be noted. Near Calva, the recent shingle beach reaches 5 feet above high-water mark and is followed by older shingle belonging to the 35-foot raised beach. At Port an Fhir-bhreige, at the south end of the island, there is a remarkable deposit of ungrassed shingle rising to nearly 30 feet above high-water mark.

The island reached its present elevation above the sea some time after the advent of man into the British area.

The surface of Iona at the present day is diversified by rocky knobs, hillocks, and ridges, running more or less in the direction of the main length of the island, giving a topography of great variety and reproducing on a diminutive scale many aspects of Highland mountain scenery. Rocky cliffs, promontories, and islets, characterise the southern, western, and northern coastlines, facing the open ocean, with a wide, sandy bay at the beautiful plain of the Machair ; the more sheltered eastern coast, bordering the Sound, has a more even outline. Some of the "slocs" along the coast have been eroded by the sea along the course of igneous dykes, though others owe their origin to marine erosion along joints or cracks. Differential erosion by the sea is responsible for the hollowing out of recesses, clefts, and caves, around the coast. During storms many tons of water are poured suddenly into a cleft, causing compression of the air in the joints at the far end, and, on retiring, exerting suction with the result that from time to time parts of the wall or roof are brought down. An inland passage may thus be gradually formed by the sea giving rise to a "blow-hole" or "puffing-hole" through which spouts of foam and spray are thrown high into the air. The Spouting Cave on the west coast, south of the Machair, is a striking example.

The inland cliff at the south-west corner of the island running from Port Beul-mor to Port Aoineadh nan Sruth is probably a *fault* scarp.

An area of blown sand uncovered by vegetation ("The White Sands") occurs at the north end of Iona, consisting largely of comminuted shell debris. It possibly owes its origin partly to the action of winds on the pre-existing material of an adjacent raised beach. Other areas of blown sand are found on the western coast, and the Machair with its beautiful cover of green turf is underlain by similar shell debris.

In the bays on the southern and western coasts the action of the waves has yielded beautifully coloured pebbles of which the most famous is known as the Iona Pebble. This is found on the shore at St Columba's Bay. It is a pretty, green variety of serpentine varying in colour from darkish green to light-greenish yellow. The pebbles are probably derived from serpentine nodules in an under-sea extension of the Iona Marble, and are thrown up on the beach during storms.

The lonely and shallow tarn of Staonaig is the only loch in the island, and it lies in a hollow of the gneiss on the southern plateau. Lochan Mor, to the south of Dun I, marks the site of an artificial sheet of water now dry and drained by a small stream making its way to the sea past the north side of the Cathedral buildings. The water supply of the island is obtained from a number of good springs. There is no peat on the island, and there are no trees except a few on the sheltered eastern side near the Manse.

REFERENCES.

Professor T. J. Jehu—"The Archæan and Torridonian Formations and the Later Intrusive Rocks of Iona." (*Trans. Roy. Soc. Edin.*, Vol. LIII., Part I., No. 8, 1922.

Mem. Geol. Surv. Scot.—"The Geology of Staffa, Iona, and Western Mull." 1925.

APPENDIX

PLACE-NAMES

The following interpretations are necessarily brief. *Ach a' bhathaich* alone calls up a vision of monastic activities. If one or two of the translations seem far-fetched or inappropriate, it must be remembered that the Celtic imagination is sometimes whimsical, that Pagan and other customs have disappeared, and that in a few cases even the physical features of the land have altered much with the passage of time.   D. M. F.

Ach a' bhathaich.   Field of the byre.
A' cham-a-leoib.   The bent or curving lip (inlet).
A' charraig fhada.   The long rock.
A' cheapaich.   The tillage-plot.
A' chlach mhor.   The big stone.
A' chorrag.   The (fore)finger.
A' ghlaic mhor.   The big defile or hollow.
Airde, ard ; ard.   Height ; promontory, high.
Allt a' chaorainn.   Cliff of the rowan (R.).
Am baile mor.   The big township (Iona village).
A' mholldrunach.   The pebbly beach (for m. dornach).
An ailean bhàn.   The fair sward.
An Aird.   The height.
An curachan.   The wee-coracle.
An geodha dearg.   The red creek.
An goirtean dubh.   The black little-cornfield.
An òs.†   The river (or sea) mouth (Traigh Mhor orig.).
Ardionra (by-form of Ard-annraidh).
Aodann an taoibh aird.   Face of the high side.
  ,,   an lochain.   Face of the lochlet.
Aoineadh an taghain.   Cliff of the marten-cat.
  ,,   mor.   Big cliff.
  ,,   nan sruth.   Cliff of the streams.

Ard an dobhrain.   Otter's point.
  ,,   -annraidh.   Height of storm.
  ,,   nan tighean.   Height of the houses (? taghan, of the martens).
Atha, an.   The kiln.
Athaluim.†   Bare plain.

Bealach bàn.   White (fair) pass.
  ,,   bristeadh toin.   Pass with abrupt ending.
  ,,   gaoithe.   "Windy goul."
  ,,   grulainn.   Pass of stony ground.
  ,,   mor, am.   The big pass (gap).
  ,,   na leacaich.   Pass of the *leacach*, *q.v.*
  ,,   nam băn.   Pass of the women.
  ,,   nan luirgean.   Pass of the shanks (ridges).
  ,,   nan tuilmean.   Pass of the knolls.
  ,,   Phaidein.   Little Pat's pass.
  ,,   sgreige.   Pass of rocky ground.
Beul builg.   Mouth of the inlet (bag). loc. Bellows' mouth.
  ,,   mor, am.   The big mouth or opening.
Blar an fhiona.   Plain of the wine.
  ,,   a' phubuil.   Plain of the tent.
  ,,   buidhe.   Yellow plain.
  ,,   nam manach.   Plain of the monks.
  ,,   odhar.   Dun-coloured plain.

Bol leithne. Buaile? Eithne. Eithne's fold.

Bruthas, am. The brew (mixture or "mess").

Bruthach an rois. Ascent of the rose (-bush).

,, na ceapaich. Ascent of *a' cheapaich, q.v.*

Buaile nan cailleach. Fold of the old women (? nuns).

,, nan caorach. Pasture of the sheep.

,, nan geodh. Pasture of the geese.

,, Staonaig. Fold of Staonaig.

Buailidh or Buaile Phaidein. Little Pat's fold or pasture.

Buidhneach. (The) place of yellow flowers.

Caibeal Muire. (St) Mary's Chapel.

Calva (a holding named after Eilean *Chalbha*).

Camus Cul an taibh. The bay at the back of the ocean, or ? *Cuildamh* bay.

Caol or Caolas annraidh. Strait of Storm.

Caolas na h-Aird. Strait of the *Aird*.

Carn buidhe. Yellow rocky-hill.

,, Cul ri Eirinn. Cairn of (the) back to Ireland.

,, Leth an rathaid. Half-way rock or cairn.

Carraig a' chaolais. Rock of the strait.

,, a' mhuiltein. Rock of the little wether.

,, an daimh. Rock of the ox.

,, Ard-annraidh. Rock of Ard-annraidh, *q.v.*

,, Druim-Dhughaill. Rock of Dugald's ridge.

,, 'ic Guaire. Macquarrie's rock.

,, na feannaig. Rock of the hoodie-crow.

,, Tra' an t-suidhe. Rock of *Tra'*, etc., *q.v.*

Ceann Aindrea. Andrew's headland.

,, an uird. Head of the hammer.

,, na creige. Head of the rock.

,, -Sear (an). (The) East End.

Chnotag, a' The mortar-rock.

Chorr sgeir *a muigh*, a'. The *outer* extra (or pointed) skerrie.

,, sgeir *a stigh*, a'. The *inner* extra skerrie.

Cill (cladh) Chainnich.† Cell or chapel (graveyard) of (St) Kenneth.

Cill mo Neachdain.† Cell (afterwards *cladh*) of my Nechtan.

Cill mo Ghobhannan.† Cell of my Gobnenn : orig. a pagan god.

Clacha dubh, na.† The black stones.

Clachanach. Place of stones.

Clachan corrach. Wobbly (or pointed) stones.

Clach nan laogh. Stone of the calves.

,, staoin. Inclining stone (R.).

Cladh na meirghe. Burying-place of the banner : "where unbaptised children used to be buried" (R.).

,, an Diseirt. Burial-ground of the "Desert" or Hermitage.

,, Iain (= Cladh an diseirt). (St) John's Graveyard.

,, nan druineach. Graveyard of the craftsmen.

,, Ronain. (St) Ronan's churchyard.

Clais domhain. Deep gully.

Cnoc a' bhodaich. Hill of the old man.

,, -a-chnamh. Hill of the bones.

,, a' choilich. Hill of the cock.

,, -a-chno. Nut hill.

,, an aon bhealaich. Hill of the single gap.

,, an fhiona. Hill of the wine.

,, an fhaing (chaoil). Hill of the fank (narrow).

,, an òis. Hill of *An òs, q.v.*

,, an ruamhair. Hill of the digging.

,, an teanganaich. Hill of the tongues.

,, an tobair. Hill of the well.

,, an t-suidhe. Hill of the seat.

,, aobhrain. Hill of the mass (R.).

,, Bàn. White hill.

,, buidhe. Yellow hill.

,, "beul-mor." Hill of Beul-mor.

,, briste. Broken hill.

,, bristeadh chlach. Hill of stone-breaking.

,, cas. Steep hill.

,, Ceann an locha. Kinloch (loch-head) hill.

,, chaman. Hill of the bends (loc. shinty sticks).

,, Cheann an amair. Hill at the head of the trough.

,, Ciarain. Hill of Ciaran (the swarthy one).

,, Cuil-Phail. *Cùil-Phail* hill.

,, daraich. Hill of the oak.

,, driseach. Brambly hill.

,, dubh. Black hill.

,, Earrann na sgillinn. Hill of the penny portion-of-land ? ?

,, fada. Long hill.

,, loisgte. Burnt hill.

Cnoc leathan. Broad hill.
,, meadhoin. Middle hill (at Clach-anach).
,, mor. Big hill.
,, mor nan gall. Big hill of the strangers.
,, na losgainn. Hill of the frog.
,, na bearna. Hill of the gap.
,, na carcuil (=carcair). Hill of the cell (or prison (R.)).
,, na claiginn. Hill of the rich-soil.
,, na cloiche (now Cnoc meadhoin, above). Hill of the stone.
,, na corra-chosaig. Hill of the taper-nook.
,, na criche. Hill of the boundary.
,, na faire. Hill of the watching (=look-out hill).
,, na h-analach. Hill of the panting.
,, na maoile buidhe. Hill of the yellow bare-hill (a duplicate).
,, nam bradhan (mor, beag). Hill of the querns (big, little).
,, na h-uinneig (R.). Hill of the window (R.).
,, nam bo. Hill of the cows.
,, nam bothan. Hill of the bothies.
,, nam buachaillean. Hill of the herdboys.
,, nam marbh. Hill of the dead.
,, na meirghe. Hill of the banner or signal.
,, na mòna. Hill of the peat-moss.
,, (nan) aingeal (Colliculus angel-orum). Hill of (the) angels (now an Sithean mor).
,, nan carnan. Hill of the rocks.
,, nan caorach. Hill of the sheep.
,, nan cliabh. Hill of the creels.
,, nan dias. Hill of the corn-ears.
,, nan glac. Hill of the hollows.
,, (nan) druidean. Hill of (the) starlings.
,, Odhrain. (St) Oran's hill.
,, Ruaraidh. Rory's (Roderick's) hill.
,, urrais. Hill of surety (R.). Pre-ferably, Hill of the Brownie (ùraisg).
Cnocan an aiteil. Knoll of the "blink" (? juniper).
,, na Buidhneich. Hillock of Buidh-neach (q.v.).
,, sguthaman. Hillock of (the) stacks.
,, fiar. Crooked hillock.
Cnotag. See Chnotag.
Cobhain Cuildich †=Cabhan cuilteach. Retired hollow (The Hermit's cell).
Coire sianta. Charmed (sacred) corrie or hollow.

Corr-eilean. Outstanding or pointed island ; or extra-island (adjunct to Eilean a' chlarsaich).
Creagach. Place of rocks.
Creag ghrugach. Frowning rock.
Crois. Cross.
,, Adhamhnain†, Bhriannain†, Eoin, Mhartainn, Mhic-illeathain. Cross of Adamnan, Brendan, John, Martin (Sts.), of Maclean.
Cuil-damh. Ox-shelter or -nook.
Cuil-Phail. Paul's retreat.
Cul a' claidh. (Park) behind (or back of) the burying ground.
,, na cloiche. (Park) behind the (grave) stone.
,, an Duin. (Field) behind the Dun (Fort).
Culbhuirg. (Farm) behind the Borg (Fort).

Dabhach. The vat (for steeping lint).
Dearg-phort. Red port : in Mull.
Dig (mhor). (Big) ditch.
,, na Machrach. Ditch of the Machair.
Draoighnean. Thorny ground.
Dubh-chorr. Black projection or point.
Dubh-sgeir. Black skerrie.
Druim an aoinidh. Ridge of the cliff.
,, Dhughaill. Dugald's ridge.
,, an fhaing. Ridge of the fank.
,, na cruaiche. Ridge of the heap (mound).
Dùn-Bhuirg. Dun of (the) Borg (=fort), lit. Fort-Fort—a duplicate, as in Knockhill, Barrhead, etc.
Dun Chalbha. Dun of Calva.
,, I, or Idhe. Dun (or Hill-fort) of Iona.
,, Lathraichean. Dun of (the) ruins, or sites.
,, Mhanannain. Fort of Manannan (R.). "Manannan" orig. a pagan god.
,, nam manach. Fortress of the monks.

Eaglais mhor, an. The big Church, the Abbey.
Ealadh, an. The mound or barrow (at Martyrs' Bay).
Earrann nic Lachlainn. Lachlan's daughter's portion.
Eilean a' chaolais. Island of the strait.
,, a' chlarsaich (a' chlarsair (R.)). Harp-Island (Harper's Id.).

Eilean annraidh. Island of storm (loc.
   Eilean fhionn-thra', Island of (the)
   white shore).
,, breac. Speckled island.
,, carrach. "Rough-skinned" island.
,, a' charbaid. Island of the jaw.
,, Chalbha. Island of Calf-island
   (Norse)—a duplicate.
,, didil. Island of protection (a
   breakwater), orig. *didein*.
,, dubh. Black island.
,, dunagan. Island of hummocks.
,, Lucais. Luke's island.
,, "Maol - Mhartainn." Island of
   (St) Martin's follower.
,, Mhic-an-Aba. Island of Macnab
   (Abbot's son).
,, mor. Big island.
,, Mùsimul=Mūs-holm by meta-
   thesis. (Norse)=Mouse island.
,, na h-aon chaorach. Island of the
   one sheep.
,, nam băn. Island of the women
   (the nuns).
,, nan con. Island of the dogs.
,, nan slat. Island of the tangles.
,, Phort-a'-churaich. Island of Port-
   a'-churaich.
,, rabach.† Stormy ("dirty") island
   (=Eilean annraidh).

Fang caol. Narrow fank (pen for
   sheep, etc.).
,, dubh. Black fank.
,, Mairi. Mary's fank.
,, Mhaolain. Moylan's or Baldy's
   fank. (Maolan=bald one.)
,, nan laogh. Calves' fank.
,, tigh Ghorraidh. The fank by
   Gorrie's house.
Fàradh (Fàireadh). The Eminence :
   sky-line.
Far bheann † (=Faradh). Outer or
   front peak.
Fionn-phort. White port : in Mull.

Garadh Dhiarmaid. Diarmad's garden
   (enclosure).
,, dubh Staonaig. The black dyke
   of Staonaig.
,, Eachainn oig. Young Hector's
   garden.
,, sgolban. Enclosure of thorns or
   pointed sticks (?).
,, geal. White enclosure.
,, mor. Big garden.
Gart na liana. Corn-field of the meadow.

Geodha Cnoc-a-chno. Nut-hill creek.
,, Ruaraidh. Rory's creek (where
   he perished).
Glac a' chulaidh. Dell of the boat (part
   of Lag odhar).
,, a' phubail. Dell of the tent.
,, Bhaldi. Baldy's hollow.
Glas domhain. See Clais.
,, -eilean (Glais'lean). Green island.
Gleann an teampuill (also called Gleann
   Culbhuirg). Glen of the temple or
   stone-church.
Glughtraichean, na. The well-watered
   spots (?).
Goirtean beag. Little corn-field.
,, Iomhair. Ivor's corn-field.
Grianan. Sunny spot.

I Chaluim-Chille. Iona of Columba of
   the church or churches.
Iodhlann chorrach. Tapering or pointed
   hill.
Iomair an tàchair. Ridge of the causeway.
,, cha 'n iomair (sgeir). A skerrie,
   passable at high tide. Lit. Row,
   you can't row.
,, nan Achd. Ridge of the acts or
   statutes.
,, nan righ.† Ridge (mound) of the
   Kings.

Lag an dobhrain. Hollow of the otter.
,, nan gigean. Hollow of the thistles.
,, "Beul-mor." Beul-mor hollow.
,, Labhrainn. Laurence's hollow.
,, odhar. Brown hollow.
Lamh odhar. Brown hand.
Lathraichean. Ruins or sites.
Lathullt (Leth-allt). A rocky face (lit.
   half-cliff).
Leac or Liochd. Flag-stone or flat
   ledge.
Leacach. Place of flag-stones.
Liana a' gheoidh. Meadow of the
   goose.
,, an tairbh. Meadow of the bull.
,, Chalbha. Calva lea.
,, Mhic-chulaich. Macculloch's lea.
,, mhor (nan ard). The big meadow
   (of the heights).
,, na h-uilidh. Meadow of the
   treasure.
,, nam murlach. The meadow of
   the dog-fishes (?). See Port na
   murlach.
Liochd lathraichean. Flag-stone of
   (the) ruins. See Leac.

Liochd Port a' churaich. Flat-rock of Port a' churaich.

Lochan a' mhanaich.† Lochlet of the monk.

,, na croise.† Lochlet of the cross.

,, a' bharr ruaidh.† Loch of the red point.

,, 'ic an aoig (? a man's nick-name). Lochlet of Mac-Death (cf. Mac-na-mollachd).

,, mor, an. The big lochlet or tarn.

,, liana nan curracag. The loch of the meadow of the lapwings.

Loch Staonaig. Loch of Staonaig, q.v.

Lón nam manach. Meadow of the monks.

Machair (a' Mhachair). Lowland-plain (the Machair).

Maol (a' Mhaol). The brow of the hill.

,, an aoinidh. Brow of the cliff.

,, buidhe. Yellow hill-brow or hill.

,, Chalbha. The hill (rising ground) of Calva.

,, na ciche. Pap-shaped hill.

,, nam manach. Hill of the monks.

,, nan druineach. Hill of the workers.

,, nan uan. Hill of the lambs.

,, Phaidein. Little Pat's hill.

Moel-blatha.† "Flat stone of division."

Murlugh for muirbholg. A "bag" or inlet of the sea (Irish Murlough).

Murlugh ard. Lit. High inlet, now pasture.

,, iseal. Lit. Low inlet, now pasture.

Na crossan mora.† The big crosses.

,, h-àbhain (àbhaidhean). The hollows or ups and downs.

,, h-uchdaichean. The slopes.

Nead a' ghille ruaidh. Nest of the red (haired) lad.

'Nòs †=an òs, q.v.

Poll a' bhaile. The village pool or anchorage.

,, 'dùnain. Pool of the small dùn.

,, dubhaich. Dark or gloomy pool =spongy soil.

Pollarain, pronounced Poll'areen, with accent on Poll. Place of pools. (Pool of Ireland (Eirinn) is therefore inadmissible).

Port a' chroisein.† Port of the little cross (Adamnan's).

Port a' churaich. Port of the coracle.

,, Adamnan (Adhamhnain). Port of Adamnan.

,, a' ghoirtein bhig. Port of the goirtean beag, q.v.

,, a' mhuilinn. Port of the mill.

,, an aoinidh. Port of the Uny or cliff.

,, an Diseirt. Port of the "Desert." Hermitage-port.

,, an duine mhairbh. Port of the dead man.

,, an fhir bhreige. Port of the false man, i.e., the stone near it looks like a man.

,, an t-sruthain. Port of the little stream.

,, Aoinidh an taghain. Port of the cliff of the marten.

,, Aoinidh-nan-sruth. Port of the Uny of the streams (well-watered).

,, bàn. White port (Fair-port).

,, beag na sligeanaich. The little port of Sliginach.

,, "Beul-mor." Beul-mor port.

,, Carnan a' ghille. Port of the rock of the young lad.

,, Ceann a' gharaidh. Port at the end of the enclosure.

,, Ceann an uird. Port of "Ceann-an-uird."

,, Charraig-an-daimh. Port of the ox's rock.

,, Cheann-Aindrea. Port of Andrew's point or head.

,, Chlacha geal (dubh). Port of (the) white stones (black).

,, Dunagan. Port of (Eilean) Dunagan.

,, Ghealtain. Port of Gealtan (the coward—nickname).

,, Goirtein Iomhair. Port of Ivor's corn-field.

,, Grulainn. Port of stony-ground.

,, Lathraichean. Port of (the) ruins.

,, lobha. Port of rotting (seaweed).

,, Mhurlugh cànain (for charnan). Port of the rocky inlet (?).

,, na cloiche. Port of the stone.

,, na Frainge. Port of France (French port).

,, nam mairtear. Port of the martyrs—"Martyrs' Bay." Mairtear is said to be a corruption of martira or martra (relics).

,, na muinntir. Port of the Community (the monks' port).

,, nam murlach. Port of the dogfishes.

Port nan allt beag. Port of the small streams.
,, Pollarain. *See* Pollarain.
,, Ronain. Ronan's port.

Reilig Odhrain. Oran's churchyard.
Ru' (=Rudha) a' bheoil mhoir. Point of the Beul-mor, *q.v.*
,, a' chosgarnaich. Point of the kite.
,, an eisg mhoir. Point of the big fish.
,, Mhic-aoidh. Mackay's cape, Mull.
,, na carraig geire. Point of the sharp rock.
,, na clachanaich. Point of the stony-ground.
,, na h-aird. Point of the Aird.
,, na sligeanaich. Point of Sliginach.
,, Phort - na - frainge. Point of French-port.
,, Phort - nam - mairtear. Point of Martyrs' Bay.
Ruanaich. Place of red flowers (*cf.* Buidhneach).

Sgeir. A rock *in the sea.* (Norse)
S. bheag=little skerrie.
,, aithne. Liver (shaped) rock.
,, Chaesar. Caesar's (?) skerrie.
,, eighe. Serrated rock.
,, fhir Thiridh. The Tiree man's skerrie.
,, leathan (mhor). The broad (large) skerrie.
,, Mhic Caluim. MacCallum's skerrie.
,, na caoineig (? cuinneig). Rock of the weeper or sea-kelpie (? pail).
,, nam mart. Rock of the cows (landed here).
,, ruadh. The red rock.
,, Uilleim. William's rock.
Sgeirean bhun-an-uisge. Skerries of the water-foot.
Sgurr an fhithich. The raven's peak.
,, beag. Little peak.
,, mor. Big peak.
Sithean beag. Little fairy-mound.
,, mor. Big fairy-mound.
,, mor na h-aird. Big fairy-mound of the Aird.
Sliabh meadhonach, an. The middle "Sliabh" or high moorland.
,, siar, an. The western high moorland.
Sligeanach. Shelly ground.
Sloc a' gharaidh ghil. Hollow (cave) of the *garadh geal.*
,, bo Phaidein. Gully of Pat's cow.

Sloc Cheann an amair. Gully at the head of the trough.
,, dubh. Black gully.
,, Dun Mhanannain. Gully of Dun Mhanannan.
,, 'ille Bhranain. Gully of little Bran's lad.
,, na bo duibhe. Gully of the black cow.
,, na caillich-oidhche. Gully of the owl.
,, na ceardaich. Gully of the tinkers' resort.
,, nam ball. Gully of the tangles (?).
,, nam maighteach. Gully of the shells (?).
,, nam muc. Gully of the pigs.
,, nan lunn. Gully of the staves.
,, Srath Mugain. Gully of little Mungo's strath. Mugan=wee slave.
Sraid or straid nam marbh. Street of the dead.
Srath dubh. Dark strath.
Sron iolaire. Eagle's nose.
Sruth a' mhuilinn. Stream of the mill.
Stac-a'-Chorr. "Stack" of the Corr (eilean).
,, an aoinidh. Stack of the cliff.
,, liath, an. The grey stack.
,, Mhic Laomainn. MacLamont's stack.
Staonaig. Inclining ground (R.).

Teampull Ronain. Ronan's Church.
Teanga mhea'nach, an. The middle tongue.
'Tiochdal=an Tiochdar. Lower part (of the cliff).
Tigh an easbuig. House of the bishop.
Tobar Cheathain. Well of Ceathan or Kian.
,, Glac a' chulaidh. The well at the Dell of the boat.
,, magh luinge or lunga. Well of the ship plain.
,, na gaoithe tuath. Well of the north wind.
,, na h-aoise. Well of age.
,, Odhrain.† Oran's well.
Ton a' mhanaich. Hump of the monk.
Torr Abb (Aba). Abbot's torr or hillock.
,, 'lochain. Torr of the lochlet.
Tra' an t-suidhe. (Tra' is for Traigh.) Shore of the seat.
,, ban nam manach. White strand of the monks.
,, na criche. Strand of the boundary.
,, nan siolag. Strand of the sand eels.

Traigh mhor (Tra' mor).   Big strand.
Traill a' ghairt.   Trough of the corn-patch or enclosure.

Uamh a' bhodaich.   Cave of the old fellow.
  ,,   an t-seididh.   Cave of the blowing = The Spouting Cave.
  ,,   a' chroisein.   Cave of the little-cross.

Uamh na Caisge.   Cave of Easter.
  ,,   nan calman.   Pigeons' cave.
  ,,   nan sgarbh.   Cormorants' cave.
Uiridh riabhach, an.   The dappled bed or dell.
  ,,   an eich ghuirm.   Bed (couch) of the dark-grey horse.
  ,,   nam braonan.   Bed of the earth-nuts.

CORRIGENDA

An òs.†   Delete "orig."   The *òs* was more extensive than the *Traigh Mhor*.
Cnoc na corra-chosaig.   Read "Hill of the *slater*"—a flat creature found under stones.
Glac a' chulaidh.   Read "a' choilich,"—"of the cock."   So also in Tobar Glac a' chulaidh.
Iodhlann chorrach.   Read "hills"—resembling a stackyard (iodhlann)